HUGGING

by Annetta Dellinger
illustrated by Jenny Williams

THE
CHILD'S
WORLD

ELGIN, ILLINOIS 60120

Distributed by Childrens Press, 1224 West Van Buren Street, Chicago, Illinois 60607

Library of Congress Cataloging in Publication Data

Dellinger, Annetta E.
  Hugging.

  (What is it?)
  Summary: Describes hugging as a way to say "I love you," "I forgive you," "I need you," and other expressions of emotion.
    1. Children's stories, American.   [1. Hugging—
Fiction]   I. Williams, Jenny, 1939-   ill.
II. Title.   III. Series.
PZ7.D385Hu 1985   [E]   84-21505
ISBN 0-89565-301-X

HUGGING

What is hugging?

Hugging is putting your arms around
someone . . . and more. It makes you
feel . . . happy, special, warm, tingly,
joyful, but most of all, loved.

Hugging is a way to say, "Hi! I'm
glad you are home."

Hugging is a way to say, "Good-by.
I'll miss you."

Hugging is a way to say, "I love you because you are my family."

Hugging is a way to say, "Thank you
for all the nice things you do."

When accidents happen, hugging is a
way to say, "I forgive you."

When you have been mean to someone, a hug will say, "I'm sorry."

When you hear thunder and see light-
ning, Dad's hug says, "I'm here."

Does a T.V. show scare you? Mom's
hug says, "It's okay. I understand."

Have you been sick? Your friend's
hug says, "I'm glad you are feeling
better."

Did you cut your finger? Sister's
hug says, "I know it hurts."

Hugging says, "I'm so glad you've
come!" when Grandma visits from far,
far away.

Hugging says, "I need you," when
just Grandpa and you are fishing.

Hugging says, "I'll be thinking of you," when your best friend moves away.

Hugging says, "I like you just the way you are," even when your two front teeth are missing.

When big brother sticks up for you,
a hug says, "I'm glad I have you."

When you have a good paper,
a hug says, "I'm proud of you!"

Hugging says, "I'll help you, just because I love you."

25

Hugging is a way to say, "Have a great day!"

Hugging is a way to say, "Good night.
I'll see you in the morning!"

Hugging is free. It can be done at
any time, for any reason . . . or for
no reason at all.

Hugging is putting your arms around
someone . . . and showing you care.

Can you think of other reasons for hugging?

About the Author:

Annetta Dellinger has authored numerous children's books, curriculum guides, and teachers' helps, and is a published free-lance photographer. Majoring in education, Mrs. Dellinger attended Wittenburg University, Ohio University, and Bank Street College in Washington, D.C. Currently she is director and teacher at Trinity Pre-Kindergarten in Marysville, Ohio, and is Early Education Consultant for the American Lutheran Church, Minneapolis. She also conducts teacher and leader workshops. Mrs. Dellinger and her husband live in Plain City, Ohio, with their two teen-age children.

About the Artist:

Jenny Williams is a graduate of Wimbledon College of Art and London University Institute of Education. For several years she worked as a commercial artist. More recently she has been kept busy illustrating for children, her favorite work. An ex-Londoner, Mrs. Williams has lived for the past ten years, as she says, "deep in the wild heart of Wales." She is the mother of two preschool children, she reports, who also "enjoy painting—particularly their faces."

3

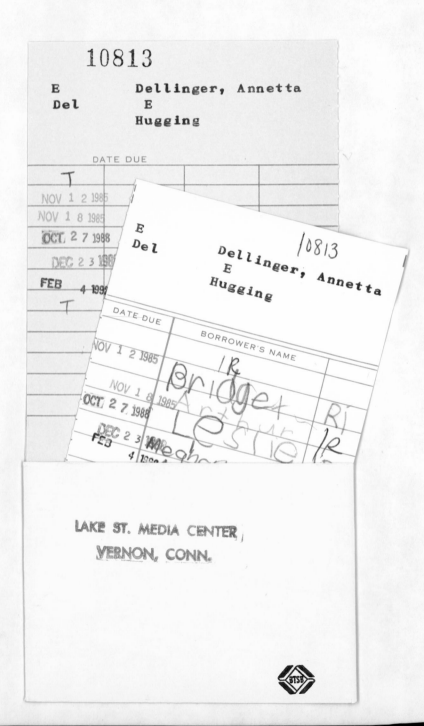